THE TALE OF TOM

For Julian and Evan,

You may not remember it, but you were fortunate to
see Tom play. I hope you both follow your passions
and always make time for play.

And for the children of New England,

I hope this book helps you understand why Tom
Brady was so special. You've been born into the
greatest sporting culture in the world. Make sure you
appreciate every championship as if it was your last.

IBSN: 978-0-578-83270-8 (Hardcover)
ISBN: 978-0-578-83308-8 (Paperback)

First Edition

Printed in the United States

10 9 8 7 6 5 4 3 2 1

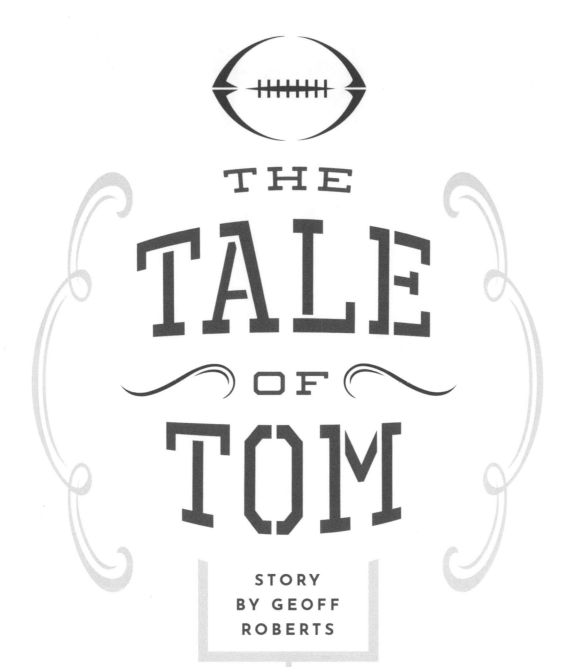

THE
TALE
OF
TOM

STORY
BY GEOFF
ROBERTS

Illustrations by Tracy Lynn Rabago

CONTENTS

CHAPTER I:

A LEGEND IS BORN

At the beginning of the millenium,
when your parents were young
Watching New England sports
wasn't so much fun.

The Red Sox were cursed by Babe Ruth,
they hadn't won in 80 years!
And watching the Patriots play football
didn't lead to many cheers.

The Patriots had never won a Super Bowl,
but that would all change in 2001!
When a skinny kid named Tom Brady,
settled into shotgun.

Thomas Edward Patrick Brady Jr.
was born on August 3, 1977.
His mother didn't know it yet,
but she'd delivered a slice of heaven.

Little Tommy grew up a California kid,
living by San Francisco Bay.
Baseball! Basketball! Football!
His afternoons were spent at play.

He'd practice and practice,
perfecting his pass.
And soon earned himself a spot
in Michigan's recruiting class.

CHAPTER II:

UNDERDOG

When Tom arrived in Ann Arbor,
he struggled to even make the team.
But he kept working hard,
taking small steps towards his dream.

He'd start and play well,
his Junior and Senior year.
But his chances of making the NFL
were still anything but clear.

The 2000 NFL draft finally came,
days which would decide Tommy's fate!
Player after player was selected—
Tom feared it was getting too late.

The scouts said he was too skinny.
He wasn't very fast!
His apprehension grew,
as team after team passed.

Six quarterbacks had been picked,
as the 6th round drew to a close
Then suddenly Tom heard his name called,
and the 199th pick rose!

Patriots coach Bill Belichick called Tom
and welcomed him to the team.
His hard work had paid off—Tommy had a
chance to live out his dream!

Over the next 20 years, a record of six
Super Bowls would be won.
Saddle up boys and girls—
this is the story of each one!

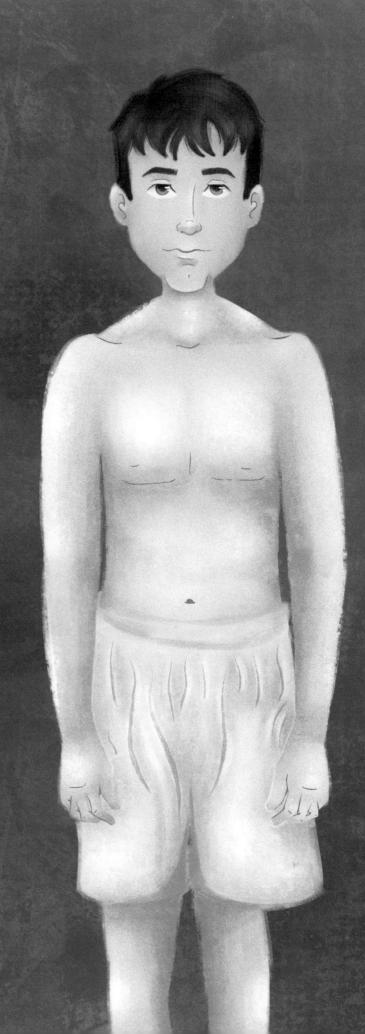

CHAPTER III

BECOMING A CHAMPION (2001)

When Tom got to Foxboro, he again
had to prove that his skills were real.
Drew Bledsoe was the quarterback,
and he'd just signed a 10-year deal.

Tom competed hard at every practice,
before approaching team owner Robert Kraft.
"I'm the best decision you've ever made," he said—
a bold statement from the 199th pick in the draft!

Everything would soon change,
in the second game of the 2001 season,
Drew Bledsoe got hurt—sometimes
everything happens for a reason!

New England fans were mad.
They'd lost their starting QB!
But Tom Brady stepped up,
recognizing his opportunity.

In football and in life,
you need to work hard and be prepared.
When Tom finally got his shot,
he was ready instead of scared.

Tom played great right away,
winning 11 games by the end of the season.
The Patriots were heating up, even though
the weather in New England was freezin!

When the playoffs began,
the Patriots continued to roll.
They faced the St. Louis Rams
in Tom's very first Super Bowl.

The Rams were a great team, nicknamed
the "Greatest Show on Turf."
But with the game tied Tom took the field,
determined to bring them back to earth.

Only 90 seconds remained!
And the Pats had no time outs!
But Tom drove them down the field,
even as Patriots fans had their doubts.

Adam Vinateri kicked a field goal
to win the Patriots the game!
And New England fans celebrated
their first Super Bowl victory,
from Rhode Island to Maine!

Tom grabbed his head as the ticker tape fell,
celebrating with glee.
It was his first Super Bowl championship,
and he was named the game's MVP.

CHAPTER IV:

BACK TO BACK
(2003 & 2004)

The 2002 season
wasn't the Patriots best,
But they'd found their new quarterback,
and would soon continue their success.

In 2003 they faced the Colts
in the AFC championship game,
Peyton Manning threw 4 interceptions,
and the Colts came up lame.

The Patriots played the Carolina Panthers,
in an amazing Super Bowl.
They pulled off the victory,
and played with heart and soul.

The game was tied late...
There was only one minute to go!
As Tom led the Patriots down the field,
completing throw after throw.

Another Adam Vinateri kick won the game!
The Patriots had continued their clutch play!
And Tom had earned his second Super Bowl
MVP, by the end of the day.

Most

MVP

valuable player

By 2004 the Patriots
were the team to beat,
They ran through the regular season,
before handing Peyton Manning another defeat.

In the AFC championship, Tom beat
the Steelers and quarterback Big Ben.
Then in the Super Bowl he threw 2 touchdowns,
finishing with a passer rating of 110.

The Eagles were defeated!
The Pats had won 3 out of 4!
They'd officially become a dynasty,
but could they win any more?

DYNASTY

dy•nas•ty | \ ‘dī-nə-stē

1 :a powerful group, family, or team that maintains its
position for a long time (see also New England, champions)

// the Patriots have become a *dynasty*.

CHAPTER V:

CAN'T WIN 'EM ALL

The next 10 years would be
Tom Brady's prime,
But suddenly winning wasn't so easy—
the 2007 Super Bowl was a crime!

That year the Patriots never
lost a game, going 16-0,
It seemed like Randy Moss caught
a touchdown, on every Tom Brady throw.

Tom set the record for the most
touchdown passes in a season with 50!
Everybody in New England
thought that was pretty nifty.

But the Pats lost the Super Bowl,
in a game that was a total fluke.
When Eli Manning closed his
eyes and launched the ball skyward,
I wanted to puke.

2008 didn't go any better—
Tom was hurt in the very first game!
And in 2011 the Patriots lost the Super Bowl again—
this time they had only themselves to blame.

CHAPTER VI:

FAMILY

Losing is tough,
but it happens to us all.
Tom kept a level head—
he knew there is more to life than football.

He'd won three Super Bowl championships—
the record was four
When I looked towards the heavens and prayed,
"Please let Tommy win one more!"

Tom knew that a 4th Super Bowl title,
would make him an all-time great.
But it was around this time,
that he agreed to a blind date.

Her name was Gisele and
my-oh-my she was pretty!
She brought out the best in Tom,
and made him act silly.

She was tall and lean,
with beautiful Brazilian skin.
Tom fell for her hard—
her heart was perhaps his greatest win!

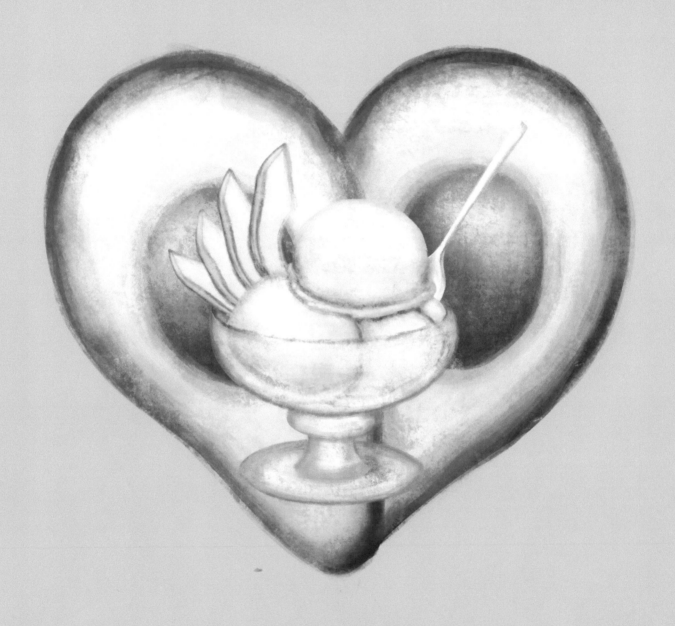

They'd sit around the house laughing,
snacking on bowls of avocado ice cream.
It had been years since the Patriots had won,
but Tom was still living a nice dream.

Gisele and Tom started a family,
raising their kids to be gentle and kind.
Tom was a family man now, but winning another
Super Bowl was never far from his mind.

CHAPTER VII:

BECOMING THE GOAT (2014)

By 2014 Tom was getting up there in age,
Reports said his skills were declining—
he was more of a quarterback sage.

The Patriots met the Seahawks in the Super Bowl,
a team with a great D.
Tom led a comeback yet again,
throwing a touchdown when
Julian Edelman broke free.

But the Pats had scored too fast,
giving the Seahawks the ball!
When Seattle drove to the 1-yard line,
it looked like the Pats would again fall.

The Seahawks needed just one itty bitty
yard to win the game,
They'd certainly run the ball,
at least if their coach was sane!

But Russell Wilson dropped back,
unleashing a short pass
Malcom Butler intercepted the ball,
and the celebration was on in Mass!

Tom jumped up and down,
his fourth Super Bowl win!
Richard Sherman could only
extend his hand to Tom,
his face looking grim.

CHAPTER VIII:

THE GREATEST COMEBACK OF ALL-TIME (2016)

In 2016 Tom's Patriots reached
the Super Bowl for the 7th time,
But late in the third quarter,
they'd fallen WAY too far behind.

Tom's mom had fallen ill, she was
watching at home with cancer.
"Let's win it for your mom!" Julian called out.
Tom knew he had to answer.

The Patriots scored 25 points in the second
half, the greatest comeback of all-time.
Tom had won it for his mom!
Raising his fifth Super Bowl trophy felt divine.

CHAPTER IX:

PERSPECTIVE

In the 2017 Super Bowl,
Tom played his very best against Philly.
His three touchdowns were great,
but his 505 passing yards were just silly.

But the Patriots didn't play defense,
letting the Eagles score 38.
They scored 33 points of their own—
even in losing Tom's performance was great.

His kids rushed the field after the game,
tears in their eyes because they'd lost.
But Tom was gracious in defeat,
refusing to be cross.

"I'm disappointed kids," he said.
"But I gave it my all!"
Sometimes that's just life... win or lose
you have to stand tall.

Tom taught us all a lesson that day,
about sportsmanship and life.
He was sad to have lost, but it was more important
to hug his kids and wife.

CHAPTER X:

THE FINAL CHAPTER (2018)

Tom would get another chance,
  the very next year against the Rams.
But this game was defined by defense—
it was even boring for the fans.

As the game wore on, Tom found Gronk
with a deep pass down the middle!
The Patriots scored the game's only touchdown,
solving the Rams' defensive riddle.

They hung on to win, the final score
a sleepy 13 to 3.
It was the last Super Bowl that Tom would win,
for Patriots fans like me.

2019 was Tom's last year as a Patriot,
but the team had no offensive threats.
Watching the playoffs was tough...
but not as bad as watching the Jets!

Tom was a great leader,
but an even better teammate and human.
He made everyone around him better,
that much has been proven.

There was Givens and Branch,
Brown, Welker and Randy Moss.
So many players were lucky,
to catch a Tom Brady toss.

Gronk Spike! Watch out! Here comes Julian
with another dazzling play.
Tom treated them all like family,
and they made each other better each and every day.

All of us in New England were blessed
to watch Tom for twenty beautiful years,
The thrill of my sporting life was watching him—
he gave us so many reasons to cheer!

The greatest quarterback to ever play football,
and the fiercest competitor in the game.
I read you this book, because I want you to
know Tom Brady's name.

THE END

ABOUT THE AUTHOR

Geoff Roberts grew up in Manchester, New Hampshire at a time when Boston sports teams were best known for losing. After a dominant Little League career, he threw out his arm as a teenager and spent the next 20 years weeping quietly to himself while watching every game of Tom Brady's career. He lives in San Diego with his wife, Kelley, and their twin sons, Julian and Evan.

CPSIA information can be obtained
at www.ICGtesting.com
Printed in the USA
BVHW020255290621
610676BV00001B/4